TH

Seeking God for the Transformation of a City

RICHMOND

BY DOUGLAS MCMURRY AND THE
TRANSFORMATION RICHMOND TEAM

© 2003 by Douglas McMurry

Published by Bethlehem Books
2508 Dickens Road
Richmond, VA 23230

Printed in the United States of America

Unless otherwise noted, all scripture quotations are taken from the
New International Version of the Bible, copyright 1973, 1978, 1984
and 1995 by Zondervan Corporation.

No part of this publication may be reproduced, stored in a retrieval
system or transmitted in any way by any means without prior
permission of the author except as provided by USA copyright law.

ISBN 0-914869-00-0

ACKNOWLEDGMENTS

This book was born out of two years of productive meetings of Transformation Richmond, a network of Christian leaders who share a common hope—that the Church in the greater Richmond area will work together, pray together and minister as fellow believers in the same Lord. This group is not a formal organization, but a network of people who have labored for a common vision in this city. In this work, we have learned to trust one another, and to stand together in support of each other. The men and women of Transformation Richmond were intimately involved in the development of this manuscript, and in the growth of the vision it articulates. If they were to write this book, no doubt, they would have written it differently. Yet they have trusted me to articulate for the team the hopes that Christ has given us all.

Therefore, I wish to thank Wayne Mancari of Cornerstone Assembly of God in Chester, Chuck Crismier of the Richmond Connection and Save America Ministries, Lyle Thomas of Christian Ministries United, Don Coleman, ambassador for Transformation Richmond, Bob Perry, Missions Team Leader of the Richmond Baptist Association of the Southern Baptist Church, Chris and Jeanine Guidry of Jesus Day, Matthew and Sherrie Moore of Common Thread, Buddy Childress of Needle's Eye Ministries, Bob Ruthazer of Marriage Builders Alliance, James Anderson of the Family Policy Council, and my very supportive friend, Jack Smith for their participation on the team and their input about the manuscript.

I also wish to thank Galen Blom of Mission Houston and CitiReach International for his invaluable advice to the team, and to me concerning this manuscript. Galen has selflessly trekked to Virginia from Texas many times as a consultant to Transformation Richmond. Lyle Thomas of Christian Ministries United was instrumental in drawing Jack Dennison and Galen Blom of CitiReach to Richmond, and instigating the whole process of forming Transformation Richmond. He is to be commended for this ground-breaking work of pulling people together to initiate the vision of a city-wide Church.

The members of my own congregation, Christ Presbyterian Church, have been helpful beyond measure in their support and practical help: John Lindner, for the typesetting and the cover, Ted Backherms for his photo of the city, Cinnie Judd and Wendy Kliewer for proof-reading, Janet Brown for legal and practical advice, and the entire church for allowing me time to complete the writing.

—Douglas McMurry

CONTENTS

Part One

THE HOPE
OF TRANSFORMATION

Chapter One

THE POWER OF GOD

Through his "Transformations" videos, George Otis, Jr. has helped millions of Christians to comprehend what can happen when God shows up in a city. Otis's worldwide research has opened many eyes to an old idea—that, rather than trying to do all God's work for Him, Christians are called to rely on His power. Otis's research, in turn, stands on top of the work of others before him—J. Edwin Orr and Iain Murray among them—who have written about past seasons of spiritual awakening.

This research has made its mark here in Richmond, Virginia. Many Richmonders are fired up with a vision to move beyond the business-as-usual efforts that churches have employed on God's behalf in past years. We are coming to believe that God wants to visit Richmond as He has visited other cities both past and present during seasons of spiritual awakening.

What Shall We Call It?

This infectious hope goes by many names.

- Some call it *revival*, to emphasize that God can give life to dying churches, then use those churches to revive a dying society.

- Some call it *harvest*, referring to the way God prepares a generation to receive Christ, then sends out laborers to gather them into the Church.

- Others call it *awakening*, to emphasize that people cannot be badgered into the Kingdom, but are awakened to Christ from within.

- Others call it *reformation*, to show how God can restructure the Church's worldview, doctrines, government, discipline, and ministries according to the original intentions of the Bible.

- Others call it *transformation*, to focus on the ultimate hope—that a renewed Church can and must have an impact on the structures and on the spiritual and moral tone of the city in which it exists.

A City-wide Focus

Whatever we may call it, God seems to be giving rise to a movement that is currently affecting hundreds of American cities. Before it reached this country, this movement had already gained credibility in other nations like Argentina. As Jack Dennison of CitiReach International writes in his book, *City Reaching,*

> *From the biblical perspective, we are reminded there is only one Church in any particular geographic area where the Body of Christ has been established. This was clearly the case with the early Church and it remains true today. Argentine pastor Carlos Mraida has written, "The city is the biblical environment that defines the local character of the church."[1]*

The New Testament churches identified themselves by their city context. To this day, we read the letters Paul wrote to "the church at Corinth" or Thessalonica or Rome.

Paul was horrified at the thought that churches would take a human being as their main source of identity, whether it be "Paul" or "Apollos" or some other Christian leader.

Yet, for good or ill, Christians are no longer horrified at this practice. We call ourselves "Wesleyans" or "Mennonites" or "Benedictines" or "Calvinists" at the drop of a hat, and think nothing of it. Even those denominations that don't use a founder's name as their identity cling to doctrinal distinctives as though they were more important than their inheritance in Christ.

These distinctives are not evil. They are often divinely appointed gifts and insights God gave through certain individuals in our past. They are to be received and appreciated with thanksgiving. But most Christians today have allowed our distinctives to become so important that we have lost the sense of our commonality in Christ.

We who now hope for the revival and transformation of Richmond propose that twenty-first century Christians return to the older practice of identifying ourselves as The Church in a particular city, while still celebrating our various distinctives in a less grandiose way. This would seem to be a necessary prelude to our main calling—to usher God's Kingdom into our city together.

God's Heart for Cities

Jacques Ellul, in his book, *The Meaning of the City,*[2] points out that, though cities are the inventions of people, God incorporates the idea of cities into His plans. In fact, the future is pictured as a city—the New Jerusalem. God does not decree a nostalgic return to the Garden of Eden. His plans are to create a new type of heavenly city, as if to say, "You want a city? I will show you how to build a city." Build it from the inside out, He might say. Make it strong in spiritual things, and think about externals later.

We are not to buy into the trite and tired idea that God hates cities, or that cities are the invention of the devil, inevitably full of corruption, vice, murder and sexual perversion. We are to believe, as Paul did, that God can redeem cities—like Richmond, Virginia. God wants to make model cities, in preparation for the New Jerusalem.

Why Not Richmond?

Many in Richmond are clinging to a hope of this sort for our city. More and more we are asking, Why couldn't God do in Richmond what He has done elsewhere as portrayed in the "Transformations" videos, or in the descriptions of the great Revivals of the past — from the great Celtic Revival of Columcille to the current movements in Africa or South America? Why not seek God to do His wonders here?

This encouraging development of faith is similar to what happened in Korea just a century ago. A handful of Presbyterian, Baptist and Methodist missionaries came together in Pyongyang and began to pray for a mighty move of God. They had been visited by a believer who had come to them from the Kassia Hills Revival in India.

There, God had used certain Welsh Presbyterians, touched by the Welsh Revival, to bring the gospel to several head-hunting tribal groups, among them, the Mizo people. Huge numbers had come to Christ in a very short time, as the Spirit of God was poured out in India. To this day, the Mizos and the surrounding tribes are almost 100% Christians. Theirs is a vibrant Christianity that has completely restructured their life together according to Christian faith, love, and godliness. Mizoram, according to many who have been there, is a sort of Christian Shangrila, a place where the love of Jesus takes its proper place at the center of all social life.[3] The missionaries in Pyongyang, discouraged by relatively poor results, caught faith from what God was doing in the Kassia Hills. They said to each other, "Does God play favorites? Let us believe that God could do for us what He is doing for them."

Soon, interdenominational prayer meetings were formed, which lasted four years, 1903-1907. Finally, the Spirit of God came with power into the Church at Pyongyang, bringing deep conviction and confession of sin.

At that time, many of the Korean nationals touched by the Spirit of God began to come together every day for prayer between 4:00 and 6:00 a.m. When they did this, they would pray at the top of their lungs all at once — and not with the usual Presbyterian, Methodist or Baptist decorum. Western missionaries could not comprehend this, because they had learned that God was a God of quietness and order. But they decided not to shut this new pattern down, and the Koreans still maintain this pattern of prayer today, be they Presbyterian, Baptist, or Pentecostal. God poured out "a spirit of grace and supplication" in a uniquely Korean pattern.

The Power of God Enters a City

As they prayed, the Spirit of God went out from the Church into the city to convert many, even atheists and hardened criminals. This is how it happened, according to Jonathan Goforth, who witnessed the whole thing:

> *A deacon, who was looked upon as almost perfect, seemed to get very uneasy as the revival progressed, and he confessed to the stealing of*

some charity funds. All were astonished, but expected him to get peace; however, he descended into deeper distress and then confessed to a breach of the seventh commandment.

A woman, who for days seemed to pass through the agonies of hell, confessed one evening in a public meeting to the sin of adultery. The missionary in charge of the meeting was greatly alarmed, for he knew that if that husband killed her he would be in accord with the Korean law. That husband in tears, went over and knelt beside his sinning wife and forgave her. How the Lord Jesus was glorified as He said to that Korean woman, "Sin no more!"

Such extraordinary happenings could not but move the multitude, and the churches became crowded. Many came to mock, but in fear began to pray. The leader of a robber band, who came out of idle curiosity, was convicted and converted, and went straight to the magistrate and gave himself up. The astonished official said, "You have no accuser; you accuse yourself; we have no law in Korea to meet your case"; and so dismissed him.

A Japanese officer at the time of the revival was quartered in Ping Yang. He had imbibed the agnostic ideas of the West, therefore to him spiritual things were beneath contempt. Still, the strange transformations which were taking place, *not only among great numbers of Koreans, but even among some Japanese, who could not possibly understand the language, so puzzled him that he attended the meetings to investigate. The final result was that all his unbelief was swept away and he became a follower of the Lord Jesus.*[4]

It was Jonathan Goforth who then carried this revival fire from Korea to his own mission field in China. There, astonishingly, revival broke out in virtually all the towns Goforth visited after that. God did, in a few years of revival, what the missionaries had not been able to do in years of arduous labor.

And now we ask, Why not Richmond? Can we believe that God would do such a thing in our city?

■ ■ ■

Chapter Two

TRANSFORMATION RICHMOND

Will the people of God transform a lost world—or will a lost world transform the people of God? What sort of transformation do we expect, or hope for?

The founder of Richmond, William Byrd II, considered himself a Christian, as did his father, who founded Westover Plantation out of his earnings at the Trading Post at The Falls (of the James River). Their thinking and attitudes are reflected in *The Secret Diary of William Byrd.*[5] This diary by the founder of Richmond was written by a man of faith, a Christian apparently. Each entry concludes with this inevitable sentence: "I said my prayers and had good health, good thoughts, and good humor, thank God Almighty." Yet the aristocratic faith of this family lacked any transforming power whatever. When reading this diary, one has difficulty pinpointing how William Byrd's faith affected him or his father in any positive way.

For example, Virginius Dabney, in his *Richmond: The Story of a City*,[6] credits William Byrd I with initiating the slave trade in Virginia, developing the tobacco trade and profiting hugely from the sale of liquor. When William Byrd II inherited Westover plantation, he became the most land-rich man on the James. Nevertheless, when he was sought out by the future city fathers seeking land on which to build a city, he refused at first to give up any land for the purpose, at any price. Land was what he lived for. The founder of Richmond was also a notorious womanizer.

Would it be unfair to suggest that the Byrd family was embedded with a strain of greed and would do almost anything to enrich themselves with more land and money— and that their Christianity did not transform them out of this condition? Rather, it seems to us that it was this condition that transformed their Christianity into a low thing unworthy of Christ. The teachings of Christ about "mammon" seem not to have made any impression on them at all. This situation only worsened with the passing of generations. William Byrd III "became an irresponsible wastrel and killed himself in 1777," says Virginius Dabney.[7]

God's Mercy In Revival

God has never given His stamp of approval to such versions of Christianity. But He has graciously brought seasons in our national history in which His Spirit moved broadly to transform people out of this condition. These seasons are well known historical eras of our past:

- The Great Awakening of 1739-1743
- The Second Great Awakening of 1799-1823
- The Finneyan Revival of 1824-1830
- The Prayer Revival of 1858
- The Azusa Street Revival of 1905, which produced the Pentecostal churches

In these moves of God, it is hard to pinpoint any time when Richmond as a city was particularly affected.

For example, Iain Murray describes in detail how the Great Awakening affected Virginia. The Presbyterians, in the person of Samuel Davies, came down from the north in 1747 and settled in Hanover county, to build two congregations, one at Pole Green and another at Providence to the west of the city.[8] Then the Dover Convention Baptists moved in from the east; it was through their ministries that many of the Native tribes east of the city came to Christ.[9] Simultaneously, the Methodists came up from Suffolk and North Carolina, establishing their Methodist societies (house churches) in great profusion south of Richmond.[10]

Yet there is little evidence that these movements found their way into Richmond. They seem almost to have been stopped cold, as if by some invisible wall around the city limits.

To this day, it is the things William Byrd planted here for which Richmond is most famous. If you are African American, you will think of the slave trade that took place at the corner of 15th and Main at Bell Tavern. If you are Native American, your chief memory of Richmond is an equally painful one: Walter Plecker, racist and eugenics devotee, using his position in the Bureau of Statistics to try to obliterate the memory and identity of Native Virginians.[11]

We keep being rudely reminded that we have a long way to go in bringing God's Kingdom to Richmond. In 1985 and in 1994, Richmond's per capita murder rate was second in the nation. At the turn of the millennium, we were greeted with the spectacle of Philip Morris executives conniving to addict the young people of the world with their product, and hiding evidence of its addictiveness. We have "the William Byrd pattern" all over again.

Cities develop inertia, "the tendency of matter to remain at rest if at rest, or, if moving, to keep moving in the same direction, unless affected by some outside force."[12] Patterns like greed or racism or moral carelessness once established in a city, tend to grow there by mutual agreement, until some "outside force" knocks that city into a different pattern, breaking the inertia.

Many of us have come to believe that it is time for God to break patterns that have grown up in Richmond from the beginning. God is the only "outside force" who can do it. Apart from God doing such a thing, we will continue in the patterns of the past. We who live in Richmond cannot change Richmond's inertia, because we are part of it. But we can invite God to do this, and we can be involved in what God then accomplishes in answer to our prayers.

It is one thing when Christians lament murder, greed, dishonesty and corruption. It is another, when God shows up in a city to cleanse the city by His holy, loving and righteous presence. He alone can bring obedience to Christ. No one comes to Christ unless the Father draws him or her. Some of us believe that it is time for a move of God in our city. We believe that Richmond is ripe for revival and transformation.

New Prophetic Encouragement

Significantly, several leaders over the past twenty years have spoken over our city that it is time for just such an intervention of God. We mention a few who seem more notable because they came from outside the country to speak those words here.

We are aware that some of our Christian readers may have trouble with the more "prophetic" of these words. But let us imagine that Jesus, the Shepherd of the sheep, is calling out to key leaders, and sending them, one after another, to give hope and encouragement to us in this particular sheep pen. The value of this encouragement does not lie in a famous "prophet," but in the fact that several people coming from opposite corners of the world spoke similar words at the same time. This is what causes us to believe that the words may come from Jesus.

Words for Richmond

Among these Christians was the Welshman Rowland Evans, Founder of World Horizons, who in 1986 saw prophetically a bridge teeming with African Americans, extending from Richmond to the Muslim countries of West Africa. Because of this vision, World Horizons has placed its American office in Richmond, and is ready to provide some of the logistical support for that bridge. Implied in this vision is that God is going to deeply convert and use as evangelists and church planters transformed African Americans from Richmond.

In May of 1995, the New Zealander John Dawson, author of *Healing America's Wounds*, said of Richmond, "The fundamental fault lines of the nation lead to Richmond… I believe there may well be a tremendous national gathering at Richmond…It's a strategic location where God wants to demonstrate something dramatic." At the same time, our own Wellington Boone added, "I believe Richmond may well become the spiritual revival capital of the world."[13]

In 1998, a word about Richmond was given by Michael Ratliff, speaking in Hampton Roads.

> *The Spirit of the Lord says, I am tipping the scales on behalf of revival… I am arresting those who are trafficking in evil. And I will begin to expose great illegalities in Richmond. Therefore pray, and rejoice in this—that I am arresting evil and loosing good. In fact, the Lord says, the city council, the city fathers and the city leaders will come to their knees*

publicly and rejoice in God answering prayer.... And behold, the Lord says, I am sending you (from Hampton Roads) and many others to Richmond. For the Lord says, what was in the Civil War in Richmond will be something in revival decidedly in the same historic measure... but greater. Every road of revival is leading into Richmond and out of Richmond. I will march into Richmond in a way of victory and triumph and rejoicing. For the Lord says, it is my doing to bring a very bright light into Richmond and make it a torch to shine brightly, shining into all areas of darkness....[14]

Shortly after the turn of the millennium, Ruth Ruibal of Cali, Colombia, who was featured in the first "Transformations" video, visited Richmond. She gave a prophetic message laced with equal parts of encouragement and warning.

Richmond is at a crossroads. This may be Richmond's last chance...I believe you have already had earlier voices sent to you, calling for unity of obedience, but you have not taken seriously what has been said. The city is deceived...You have failed the original vision for the city and the country, and God wants to resurrect that vision and bring it to pass, but it will only happen when you are desperate...This is a matter of life and death. This may be Richmond's last chance.[15]

Sobering words indeed. Words that invite a response

from the Church at Richmond.

More Than Words

God's encouragement has gone beyond words. In 1986, God showed His mighty power over Richmond. At the invitation of two pastors, Louis Skidmore and Wellington Boone, Gary Bergel of Intercessors for America came to Richmond to lead an intercessors' conference. Some 700 Christian intercessors were gathered together at St. Giles Presbyterian Church, February 9-11. The sanctuary was packed, including the balcony. Prayers for Richmond concentrated on the murder rate—Richmond had been identified as having the second highest per capita murder rate in the nation.

Five weeks later, a news article in the *Richmond Times-Dispatch* appeared, announcing that an extraordinary month-long hiatus in murders, beginning on February 9, had been baffling police. Lieutenant W. E. Harver was quoted as saying, "Whatever forces are at work to keep the murders down, I hope they keep working."[15]

The Church at Richmond had managed to produce a unified voice in prayer, led by pastors who were determined to see Richmond transformed out of its reputation as a murder capital in the nation. God had responded by cutting off murders, as a clear sign of His desire to answer the prayers of the saints.

This unique occurrence in Richmond history tells us that God desires to act with power in the Richmond

Metropolitan area. His arm is not so short that it cannot save. But He is looking for certain conditions in our city, because when God acts, He acts in response to a Church that is preparing the way for Him. That begs the question: How are we to prepare the way for a fresh manifestation of God's transforming power in Richmond?

■ ■ ■

Chapter Three

PREPARING FOR REVIVAL

Those of us who have been listening to these prophetic signs and words have begun to ask ourselves, "What would it take to have a sustained move of God that would transform a city like Richmond?" Here we can turn once again to George Otis, Jr., whose conclusions were not much different from those of J. Edwin Orr before him. As detailed in the book, *Informed Intercession*, Otis says that these elements are found in virtually every place where there has been a sustained move of God:

- Significant outpourings of prayer

- Christian unity

- Persevering leadership

We see these three elements in the New Testament.

After the ascension of Jesus from the Mount of Olives, the disciples gathered in "the upper room"—probably at the home of the mother of John Mark. There they were much in prayer and "in one accord." Probably they were obeying the words of Jesus who had told them to pray for laborers for the harvest. In this context of significant prayer, unity and persevering Apostolic leadership, God poured out His Spirit on the day of Pentecost. Their prayers had primed the pump. When it was fully primed and all was ready, the living water came up so strong that it carried them along in its powerful flow into the city. The rest of the story is told by Luke in the Book of Acts.

The necessity of prayer to produce a sustained move of God is well known by now. What is less appreciated is the role of unity among Christian leaders who are willing to persevere, clinging to a common vision of Christ's Kingdom.

The Kentucky Revival

Most true Revival movements have lasted two to three years. One notable exception to this pattern was the Second Great Awakening, which provides us with a model of the sort of thing that needs to happen in order to *sustain* a move of God in an area.

In 1799, Logan County had become a catch-basin for prostitutes, murderers, thieves—ne'er-do-wells of all sorts. If any criminal back east managed to escape prosecution, he knew he could find safe haven in Logan County.

The place earned a nickname: Rogues' Harbor.

Because of the spiritual climate there, desperation produced prayer, unity and persevering leadership among the few Christians of Logan County. The Presbyterian pastor, James McGready, organized prayer meetings with his Baptist and Methodist counterparts. He also encouraged other Americans to pray for "the worst place in America." Finally, he called for a communion service for the three fledgling congregations to celebrate their oneness in Christ.

This little communion service invited the mysterious flow of God's power into the region. According to the testimony of Peter Cartright people were drawn from miles around by the mysterious power of God. There they found preachers of diverse denominational backgrounds preaching to huge crowds. Many people would fall to the ground, convicted of their sins and crimes, crying out for mercy, repenting, rising up and being baptized. In this way, God began to tame the most lawless elements of the American wilderness.

James McGready was not the only one who was urging desperate, united prayer for revival in the U.S. A Scottish Presbyterian minister in Edinburgh named John Erskine had published a paper urging the people of Scotland to unite in prayer for "A Revival of Religion." Jonathan Edwards, a leader during the Great Awakening, was so moved when he read this paper that he published a booklet of his own, stirring Christians in this country to unite in prayer up and down the East Coast.

God was then able to sustain a movement of revival, working in co-operation with a Church that was unified, prayerful and persevering. As a result, the scope, length and influence of that revival movement has been unequalled in this country. As Iain Murray summarizes:

While its name rightly puts the Second Great Awakening in succession to the first of the 1740's, it fails to alert us to the measure in which they differed. For one thing, there was a remarkable difference in time scale. The duration of the first Great Awakening extended through three to five years at most; the duration of the second was not less than a quarter of a century...

The first reached only to the eastern seaboard and to part of the comparatively small population of the 1740's. The second was of far greater geographical extent and reached far more people.

...Referring to it as 'the great Revival', the Presbyterian writer W.H. Foote said that 'it spread over the Southern and Western, and portions of the Middle States, with a power almost terrific'.[17]

Murray also quotes Edward Griffin of Connecticut, who wrote, "I could stand at my door in New Hartford, Litchfield county, and number fifty or sixty contiguous congregations laid down in one field of divine wonders, and as many more in different parts of New England."[18]

Prayer Summits

Where a significant number of praying leaders are in place, and have developed trusting relationships of Christian love, the conditions are ripe for a sustained move of God. This awareness recently dawned on Dr. Joseph Aldrich, President of Multnomah School of the Bible in Portland, Oregon. In 1987 he asked himself, "What would it take to initiate and sustain a work of God in a specific geographical community?"

Beginning at Salem, Oregon, he began to gather together a significant percentage of pastors from communities for four-day prayer retreats. He called these gatherings Prayer Summits. Since those early years, the Prayer Summit movement has affected hundreds of communities worldwide. The underlying conviction driving the Prayer Summit movement is that prayer, unity and persevering leadership are a necessary part—the human part—in sustaining a genuine move of God in a city. We believe that Prayer Summits are an important way God is preparing our country—and our city—for a sustained revival movement.

A Two-hundred-year-old Prophecy...

Perhaps this awareness will take on greater urgency and relevance in light of an e-mail we happened to catch sight of from Charlotte, N.C., from one of the descendants of those involved in the Kentucky Revival. He, Jim Brooks, writes:

In 1796, James McGready left Orange County and moved to Logan County, Kentucky. In the year 1800, the Great Revival began....

In 1802, some of the believers in the area of McGready's churches, sensing a lapse in the revival's fervor, and fearing that it was about to end, besought God for many days and weeks, to renew and continue the revival in all of its manifestation of His mighty power. There were only a few hundred of these people, and they did not advertise what they were doing. Secretly and fervently they sought God for the revival to be renewed. After some months of intense prayer, many in those prayer bands were assured by God that just as they had been seeking God for another revival, so another one would come. They felt that the one they were in would be renewed for yet a time, as indeed it was at Cane Ridge and afterwards.

What they said was that...there would be another revival, far greater than this one, far into the future, near the end of the age. This revival would come in two waves. The first wave would surpass anything that had gone before it, even the revival that began on the day of Pentecost. The first wave of the revival would be hijacked by ministers and churches seeking to use the revival for their own purposes, seeking to add members to their churches, and to build up their kingdoms rather than God's. Because of that the first wave of the *revival, though it would last a long time, would end. The second wave would not come until a number of years later. When it comes it will surpass even the first wave in its magnitude and its fervor. It will seem as if the whole world is coming to God!*[19]

Could it be that we are nearing the initial fulfillment of this prophecy? If so, can the Christian Church of America work co-operatively to seek God's transforming power for our cities?

...And a Very Present Update

Richmond was the gateway of commerce into our country years ago. Could God be calling Richmond to be a gateway for His grace and power today? This is just what God seemed to be saying when he moved upon a Finnish pastor, Rauno Kokkola, who lived in Richmond for a sabbatical year in 1999, because he was convinced that Richmond is an Eastern gate through which the Lord wants to affect our country. He wrote:

I felt strongly that the Lord wants to unite the pastors more for common prayer. As they would lay aside their own agendas, would pray together and seek God Almighty (according to 2 Chronicles 7:14), there would come healing for the whole nation. In order for this to happen, pastors need to have a city vision rather than a particular church vision. There have been pockets of revival in different cities and areas, but God wants to touch the whole nation, not only certain regions. For some reason God has a unique purpose for the city of Richmond. There would come a revival that would touch the whole city. The key is unity; unity of pastors of different churches, movements and denominations. The bigger the harvest, the more reapers the churches will need. No one can do it alone. No church can reap the harvest alone."[20]

This is a high calling and a great challenge that now faces us—attaining and sustaining unity among leaders in the Church at Richmond.

■ ■ ■

Chapter Four

REVIVAL AND UNITY

We have stressed the importance of unity when inviting and sustaining revival movements. Yet revival itself tends to invite division; all sorts of divisive behaviors have marred revival movements in the past. In part, this is because God's powerful interventions are unpredictable and often controversial. God's thoughts, after all, are higher than ours. He can unexpectedly force issues that have lain dormant for centuries, and it is especially the unexpected elements that create controversy.

Expected Elements of Revival

There are certain elements in revival that are predictable, and which most observers would agree on. The most commonly mentioned are these:

- A return to a lifestyle of dependence on God, Father, Son, and Holy Spirit, rather than on strictly human plans and efforts.

- A return to the scriptures of the Bible as our sole guide in Christian faith and practice.

- Rejection of externals of religion and behavior, in preference to a true change of heart, leading to faith, godliness, and love.

- Conviction of sin leading to deep repentance in private and public life.

- Triumphs of evangelism, as multitudes of lost and desperate people find mercy in Jesus Christ.

- Extension of the Kingdom of God beyond the walls of the Church, to dramatically change society in all areas of life. While this does not mean that we enter utopia; still, the Kingdom of God is advanced in all areas of life including the social and political.

If revival movements would stick to these basics, or if the basics would include only the expected results, our vulnerability to disunity would be minimized. But an unpredictable God seems to add elements to each movement for which there is no precedent except in Scripture. Here lies our problem in preparing ourselves for a fresh revival movement in the twenty-first century. God's thoughts are not our thoughts. When He reveals an unaccustomed thought, it catches us by surprise and we have difficulty adapting.

Revival Squabbling

There is a saying we have often heard: "The main opponents of present revival movements tend to be the leaders of the previous ones." If there is truth in this, it is surely because the older leaders are unable to see the new thing God is doing, different from the movement they were leading. They then prejudge the new elements as "heretical," "rebellious," "satanic" or "unseemly." Let's review.

The Great Reformation was a season of revival that included all the elements listed above. But in addition to the basics, God was wanting Christians to pay attention to the offense of calling people "kings" other than Jesus Christ, and to the abuse of power that happened perennially under systems of aristocracy. It was as though He were saying to them, "If you are going to accept Jesus as your King, then you can't have other kings, nor can you be kings to others. Christ alone is Lord and King." The motto that rose up in those days was, "God alone is Lord of the conscience."

The Reformers were looking for alternative ways to govern themselves, other than hierarchy and aristocracy. Men like John Calvin and John Knox came up with alternative ways of governing churches (Presbyterian ways) and countries (parliamentary ways). Those ways eventually influenced the United States through Christian leaders like John Witherspoon (the only clergyman to sign the Declaration of Independence) and James Madison (author of the Bill of Rights).

Conservatives in those days archly defended the monarchy and the doctrine of the divine right of kings. Kings ruled with God's authority, they said. They considered the revivalists of the Reformation firebrands and fanatics. Yet most of us today would admit that God was in that revival movement, and God was bringing the world through necessary birth pangs that included two civil wars, the Cromwellian war in England and the Jacobite war in Scotland.

> *Therefore, you kings, be wise;*
> *Be warned, you rulers of the earth. (Psalm 2:10)*

Or, as George Whitefield once preached to King George II: "When the lion roars, all the animals of the jungle fall silent; and when the Lord speaks, the kings of the Earth shut their mouths."[21] Is it any wonder that such views were a bit controversial in the courts of British kings, where the king ruled the English Church by divine right — or so it was thought.

Puritans, Quakers and Street Preachers

With George Fox and the Friends Movement, God was introducing the inner working of the Holy Spirit—the idea that you could look within yourself to touch base with God, and He would actually speak with you, as He did with Jesus. There was a new stress on a personal relationship with God through the inner light and interior voice of His Spirit. This sort of inner walk with God had not been emphasized much by the descendants of the

Reformers—and less so with the passing of the years.

In this country, the "Quakers" (as they were dubbed by some) who settled in Rhode Island were viciously persecuted by the Puritans of Connecticut. Puritan ideas and proprieties were offended by the new inner-light movement of the Friends. Yet today, the idea that God's Spirit speaks to our spirits has worked its way into the Body of Christ, to become a part of the world-view of most Christians. We can thank George Fox and the Friends for their perseverance in giving that gift to the rest of us.

A similar tension mounted during the Great Awakening when "Old Side" Presbyterians resisted the "New Side" work of men like William Tennent and his family, who founded the "Log College" (Princeton Seminary). Many Presbyterians refused also to see the need for the evangelistic street preaching of John Wesley or George Whitefield, even though some of the first Scottish Reformers had been street preachers.

The Second Great Awakening

In the Kentucky Revival, God tamed the wilderness. But the taming of such a sin-sick, wild and ungodly people required strong medicine. God surprised everyone by the ungentlemanly way He dealt with the backwoods people of Rogues Harbor, throwing them to the ground with violent trembling and conviction of sin until they cried out for mercy. In this way they became aware of the power of an irresistible God. God was answering the prayers of many saints nationwide, but He was doing it in a way few expected. The pastors had to have many meetings to try to hash out what to do with these manifestations of power. Some had no stomach for this, and many criticized this violent aspect of the revival because it was different from the Great Awakening.

But the Methodists (among others) leaped into the field with relish and, more than anyone else, capitalized on this new move of God. In part this was because they had persevering leaders (Francis Asbury and the circuit riders). Also, they had structures in place to disciple multitudes of new converts (Wesley's principles for Methodist societies). The Methodists also developed new methods in their evangelism, such as the altar call. Some churches began to feel as though altar calls were not a valid way of bringing people to Christ. Why? Because they hadn't done it that way during the Great Awakening. Today, altar calls are commonly used among many groups of Christians. Today, too, small groups and house churches have become common structures for discipling new believers. These are no longer castigated as new-fangled "methods."

The Finneyan Revival

The Revival presided over by Charles Finney had all the same marks of revival listed above. But in addition, God was taking aim at the institution of slavery. Though Finney did not much preach against slavery—he usually stuck to the basic gospel—he was an ardent abolitionist. The Finneyan Revival quickly became associated with the abolition movement, as Peter Marshall and David Manuel have described in their book, *Sounding Forth the Trumpet*.[22] Abolition societies by the hundreds sprang up as a direct result of this movement. During the five years between 1832 and 1837, roughly 1,000 abolitionist societies were developed, mostly in the northern cities affected by the Finneyan Revival. What God had begun in Britain during the Clapham Awakening with William Wilberforce He continued through men like Theodore Dwight Weld in this country.

But many opposed the Finneyan Revival with its abolitionist tendencies. Lane Seminary in Cincinnati, presided over by Lyman Beecher, felt the controversy most keenly. Beecher, a leader of the Second Great Awakening, opposed the abolitionist direction that the younger generation of revived Christians felt so keenly. Much support for the seminary came from slave owners in Kentucky, just across the Ohio River. Beecher's own daughter, Harriet, was appalled at her father's moral compromise (as she believed it to be), and was inspired to write the most important abolitionist tract ever written— *Uncle Tom's Cabin*. When Theodore Dwight Weld, the most influential of the seminary students, was reprimanded by Beecher for his uncompromising views, and then expelled by the trustees, virtually the entire student class left with him, to form the nucleus of the abolition movement in Ohio. Because the aristocratic South largely broke away from the whole concept of revival at this time, the seeds were sown for the Civil War.

Azusa Street

In the Azusa Street Revival of 1905, God threw another curveball to the Body of Christ. God poured out spiritual gifts in great abundance, including the gift of tongues. This element was more or less foreign to the Church at the time. Charismatic gifts as listed in I Corinthians 12 had not much appeared among Christians since the time of early leaders like Justin Martyr, Irenaeus, Tertullian, Augustine and the Celtic Christians of the sixth century. It was hard to know how to interpret the re-emergence of these gifts, and there was much controversy about it. Yet today the majority of Christians at least recognize the validity of the manifestations of the Holy Spirit because they are scriptural. Also, charismatic and Pentecostal churches are some of the most vibrant and fastest-growing churches in the world. God was reintroducing to the Church a part of our Christian inheritance.

Most of these patterns were opposed in their day simply because they were new and did not fit with standard preconceptions of what God was supposed to do. Each had a sound scriptural basis, though there were some who did a better job of interpreting it than others. But in the end, the Body of Christ has had to adapt itself to the newness of each of God's revival movements, just because they were of God. Who can resist God?

Those Christians have been wisest who have taken the "wait and see" attitude of Gamaliel in Acts 5:38-39: "If their purpose or activity is of human origin, it will fail. But if it is from God, you will not be able to stop these men; you will only find yourselves fighting against God."

Will We Let God Have His Way?

If a new wave of revival is on its way, it seems likely that Jesus Christ the King may have some surprises up the sleeve of His long white robe. Will we be ready for them? Will we allow Him to do whatever He chooses? Will we have patience to pray about areas of confusion, enter into dialogue with Christians we don't understand, and diligently pursue Christian unity even when relationships are strained?

Unity among Christians seems to be of paramount importance to God. In that conviction, we now turn to the Book of Ephesians to make sure that our understanding of Christian unity is thoroughly rooted in Scripture.

■ ■ ■

Part Two

THE BOOK OF
EPHESIANS
AND GOD'S HEART FOR
UNITY IN CHRIST

Chapter Five

UNITY IS FROM CHRIST ALONE

And he made known to us the mystery of his will according to his good pleasure, which he purposed in Christ, to be put into effect when the times will have reached their fulfillment—to bring all things in heaven and on earth together under one head, even Christ. (Ephesians 1:9-10)

Nearly every book of the New Testament addresses the issue of unity among Christians, but the centerpiece of unity in the Bible is the Book of Ephesians. The entire book is about unity in Christ. In a systematic way, Paul tells us why unity is important and how God intends to achieve it. Those who follow Christ are not expected to come up with our own ideas and plans, but to pay attention to God's announced plan for achieving unity. Let us repeat: We are not to create plans of our own.

Let's run quickly through the letter, not stopping too

long at any one place, to get a sense of Paul's revelation about Christian unity as a whole.

Jesus the Unifier

In Chapter One, Paul sets forth the most basic point: Jesus Christ Himself is the source of any unity we may ultimately achieve. God's only plan for worldwide unity is to bring all things in heaven and on earth together under Christ. Our unity depends upon this one fact. Jesus is the Head, the Lord. Yes, Jesus came to bring "not peace but a sword" (Matthew 10:34). But that sword is a temporary interruption, caused by the fact that some will reject Christ (10:35). In the end, Christ will be acknowledged by all. Jesus is the only hope for unity and world peace because Jesus is God's choice for achieving unity. This we must be clear about from the beginning, or everything else we may say about unity will go further and further off track.

Seasons of revival tend to be suffused with Christian unity, because during those seasons, a direct encounter with Jesus Himself becomes paramount, and secondary issues fall by the wayside. Iain Murray summarizes:

> *If love is the gift of the Spirit, it follows that an eminent degree of the Holy Spirit's working will be marked by eminent degrees of love between Christians. A narrow party spirit cannot coexist with a larger giving of the Spirit whose communion extends to the whole body of Christ. Exclusive attention to denominational interests may prevail*

among Christians in a period of spiritual decline; it never does so in days of enlarged blessing.[23]

Is Unity a Bad Word?

We realize that in certain circles of Christians, unity has come to have a bad name. Today there are unity movements that spring from false hopes—from mere good intentions or even from demonic doctrines. Many cults preach unity, or have "unification" in their names. These movements cannot succeed because they are not based on the person of Jesus, nor do they seek to bring people into obedience to Jesus.

But those who would disparage the true hope of Christian unity because of human or satanic unity-inoculations are tossing away the highest hopes of the New Testament. They have allowed the false to rob them of the true.

The Seven-Fold Inheritance

Here in Chapter One Paul is telling us that we are Christians because we have received a great inheritance through Jesus Christ. It is this inheritance that unites us. So let's look at these riches that come into our lives through Christ. There are seven. Paul invites us to receive all seven blessings, to unpack them and share them with each other. They are:

- *Adoption* (verse 5): When Jesus sends His Spirit of Adoption into us, we wake up to God's fatherly love and care. Before this, we may not have been able to see God as our loving Father at all.

- *Redemption* (verse 7): We have been purchased out of slavery to sin and the just requirements of God's laws, and have been set free through Jesus' atoning sacrifice.

- *Forgiveness* (verse 7): God pardons our sin unilaterally, even before we stop sinning. He reassures people who are still trapped in unclean patterns that they need not cling to guilt and shame in God's presence.

- *A New Purpose* (verses 9-11): We are created in Christ Jesus for good works that God has prepared before we were conceived. We gain a sense of this purpose by learning how to abide in Jesus.

- *The Glory of God* (verse 12): In Christ, we see the goodness, love, justice, majesty, purity, beauty, and attractiveness of God because the "face" of Jesus reveals these qualities.

- *Eternal Salvation* (verse 13): God promises to plunge us into His ocean of love forever. The essence of eternal salvation is deep fellowship with God, with whom we have been reconciled by the death of Jesus.

- *The Holy Spirit* (verses 13-14): By God's power, we are given countless assurances that we have eternal life with Christ. These are "an earnest," bits of our spiritual inheritance given now as a promise for more of the same in the next life.

These "riches in Christ" are so important and life-changing that they outweigh the smaller concerns that may divide us. In particular, Paul says, they outweigh the most serious separation that ever divided the human race: the ancient separation between God's people (the Jews) and the *goyim* (Gentiles) who were not God's people.

■ ■ ■

Chapter Six

JESUS BRINGS OPPOSITES TOGETHER

His purpose was to create in himself one new man out of the two, thus making peace, and in this one body to reconcile both of them to God through the cross, by which he put to death their hostility. (Ephesians 2:15-16)

If Jesus is the Uniting King, He is not waiting until His return to work reconciliation among us. He has established the Church, through whom He wants to begin this work now, during the Church Age.

The Big First-Century Shocker

Paul is full of the amazement of God's Category One surprise, that God was not requiring Gentiles to become Jews before they could be Christians. God was not requiring Gentile Christians to be circumcised. Instead, Jesus was giving His seven-fold inheritance directly into the hearts of Gentiles. It was the inheritance, not circumcision, that made them God's people. This was big news.

The Gentiles had been, from time immemorial, "excluded from citizenship in Israel, and foreigners to the covenants of promise," following "the ruler of the kingdom of the air." But now God was pouring His inheritance into their ocean of paganism. This fact, which was totally unexpected to every Jew who saw it happen, was controversial, to say the least. Sometimes God does controversial and unexpected things. He acts outside everyone's paradigms. His world-view is bigger than ours.

Circumcision of the Heart

At the heart of this controversy was this issue: How will God fulfill His promise to Abraham?

God had said to Abraham, "All peoples on earth will be blessed through you" (Gen. 12:3). Then God had led Abraham to sacrifice his son, Isaac, on Mount Moriah, the very mountain where Jesus was to die 2000 years later. Abraham was performing a little prophetic drama here, with God as Director. In the process, he had to learn the pain of a dad who sacrifices his son for the sake of others He loves. God chose Abraham to walk through this scenario and identify with the pain of God—though in the end, of course, God didn't require Abraham to go through with the actual sacrifice. But God Himself went through with it when He sent Jesus up for sacrifice on that same mountain.

This, then, is the answer to how Abraham's lineage would become a blessing to all the *goyim*. Not by having all the Gentiles convert to Judaism, but by using a Jewish man as an atoning sacrifice for the Gentiles. Gentiles would not have to become Jews to enter into fellowship with the Father. Through the sacrifice of Jesus, an inheritance became possible, the seven-fold blessing of Ephesians One.

All of us identify with a people, a clan, a race, a denomination or a tribe. Paul had taken great pride in being a Jew, and he had been zealous for the traditions of his forefathers. But then he met Jesus, and became identified with Christ. It wasn't that he ceased being a Jew. But Christ and the riches of Christ had become incredibly more important to him, so the former things had become "like dung" in comparative value and importance. Cultural differences, and the divisive behavior that arises from them, also were minimized to a footnote at the bottom of the page.

Now Paul was getting linked up with Gentiles who had had the same experience he had had. The result? He was more powerfully united to them than to other Jews or Pharisees. The dividing wall between Jew and Gentile was broken.

That was a Category One surprise.

What does God do in revival? He pours out His inheritance all over again. What should the result be? Dividing walls broken.

■ ■ ■

Chapter Seven

THE CHURCH, PROCLAIMER OF UNITY IN CHRIST

His intent was that now, through the church, the manifold wisdom of God should be made known to the rulers and authorities in the heavenly realms, according to his eternal purpose which he accomplished in Christ Jesus our Lord. (Ephesians 3:10-11)

Jews and Gentiles have been brought together into the Church because God has a plan: to use this new conglomerate of people to demonstrate to satanic beings His "manifold wisdom."

God has set a table before us in the presence of our enemies. He pours out His inheritance like food—appetizers, salads, entrees and desserts. The demons are consigned to look on from the shadowy sidelines. Heartless lizards, they do not like what they see: Jew and Gentile Christians loving each other because of Jesus. The theme of Chapter Three, accordingly, is love.

Wisdom Is Unity

The *NIV Study Bible* puts it this way: "It is a staggering thought that the church on earth is observed, so to speak, by these spiritual powers and that to the degree the church is spiritually united it portrays to them the wisdom of God."

"Spiritually united?" We've been fighting each other tooth and claw for generations. Preaching against each other; gossiping the defeats of each other's lives; competing with each other for the dwindling loyalty of people who still want to be Christians. How have we been "spiritually united?"

Perhaps sensing that there would be a problem at this point in God's plan, Paul then turns and prays an Apostolic prayer. This is not the sort of prayer you and I would normally pray—"O God, heal my skin rash, prosper my church and bless our country." Paul prays for what needs to occur if we are to become the fulfillment of *God's* hopes— that we, being rooted and established in love, "may have power, together with all the saints, to grasp how wide and long and high and deep is the love of Christ..." (3:18).We can love each other only if we are connected to the love of the King. We love because He first loves us.

Why We Need Jesus Every Day

Let's face it. Our own human love is pathetic. The first time someone doesn't love us back, we're all bitter about it, vowing we'll never do anything for them again.

But Paul is praying that we will have power, not to perform healings and miracles, but *to comprehend God's love.*

How many of us pray like this? The power to comprehend God's love doesn't strike us as being in the top ten choices of the things we need. It is only when we get God's heart that we would pray like this. As Mike Bickle of Kansas City has said, Apostolic prayers are prayers God has already signed on to. All we need to do is cosign them to make them effective. They are God's will, perfectly expressed in Scripture. These are the prayers we need to be praying as we lay hold of God's heart for revival:

- A wider love—more accepting of people unlike ourselves.

- A longer love—one that endures disappointments, misunderstandings and betrayals.

- A higher love—less polluted with self-interest, lust and ambition.

- A deeper love—one that connects with people at the heart levels of pain, hope and struggle.

God is calling to the Church to manifest this kind of love, divine love, in a world where, according to God's Word, the love of most people will grow cold.

■ ■ ■

Chapter Eight

LIVE WORTHILY

Instead, speaking the truth in love, we will in all things grow up into him who is the head, that is, Christ. From him the whole body, joined and held together by every supporting ligament, grows and builds itself up in love, as each part does its work. (Ephesians 4:15-16)

Chapters Four through Six move from vision into application. Paul is now telling us how to "live worthily" to the vision of Christian unity. In Chapter Four there are three ingredients set out for us to help us in our quest for unity.

Unity: What It Takes To Get There

Ingredient One: Humility (4:1-6). "Be completely humble and gentle" (4:2). During the Great Awakening, John Wesley and George Whitefield were having a public argument. Wesley, following the teaching of Arminius, believed that salvation was a cooperative adventure between God and us. Whitefield, following Calvin, believed that salvation was entirely a result of a sovereign God choosing whom He chooses. These men published and preached broadsides against each other attempting to point out each other's "mistake" for the whole world to see.

But after several years of this behavior, they decided to stop it, to treat each other with respect, recognizing that they were working for the same ends, bringing people to Jesus. What was it that caused them to stop their public dispute? Did one of them finally convert the other to their own view? No. Each began to sense that they were living unworthily to the vision of Christ. They let go of youthful arrogance, and humbled themselves in relation to each other. Both gained the humility of Christ, the heart attitudes of Christ toward each other.

Ingredient Two: Spiritual Truth (4:7-13). God has given the Church apostles, prophets, evangelists, pastors, and teachers as a network of people through whom right teaching about Jesus can get through to the human race. This right teaching is opposed by satanic "winds"— arguments, pretensions and deceptions that obscure the truth. As a rule, these try to confuse or destroy our relationship with the King in one of two ways:

- By obscuring who Jesus is, conveying a lower, less majestic message about Jesus, so that He is unworthy of being exclusively Lord of our lives. As with the ancient doctrines of Arius, we end up with a Jesus who is merely a great human being, "like God," but not God.

- By elevating other human or spiritual beings to a level equal with Jesus, so that He must share the throne of our lives with someone else. For example, the teachings of the ancient Gnostics, recently unearthed at Nag Hammadi, are full of other spirit-beings, such as the goddess Sophia, who appears as the consort of Christ and a kind of "queen of heaven."

Since unity depends on a right perception of who the King is, doctrines about the King are important, and God has delivered these doctrines once and for all through the apostles and prophets of the Church, who provided foundational teaching about Jesus (Ephesians 2:20, 1 Corinthians 3:11).

Ingredient Three: Relational Truth (4:14-32). All of us get hurt. Some days, we can't open our mouths or walk out our front doors without inadvertently hurting someone, or being hurt. Hurt people hurt people. Pretty soon, we find ourselves enmeshed in unending conflict with people. The result? Anger. Anger. More anger.

Anger turned in on oneself becomes depression. Not a good alternative to just getting mad. So Paul's next counsel still has merit today. "Do not let the sun go down on your anger." Speak the truth to each other as truth happens. We are members of one another, so we can't turn the cold shoulder or excommunicate each other except in certain extreme situations. Don't internalize anger, but deal openly with your issues with other people, especially your hurts.

The words, "You hurt me," are some of the most honest words we can say to each other. We can say them without bitterness or condemnation, but as an invitation for reconciliation. Here are some ways to deal with anger that comes from offenses:

"I was hurt by what you said. Did you intend it the way it seemed?"

"I heard that you said _____ about me. Was this perhaps just a rumor?"

"I sense you have closed off toward me. Is there some way I offended you?"

Almost all causes of disunity in the Body of Christ can be resolved by just such straightforward (and scary) truth-speaking as this. It gently confronts sin while also correcting misunderstandings, protecting relationships and soothing hurts.

■ ■ ■

Chapter Nine

HOLINESS, HUMILITY AND SUBMISSION

Speak to one another with psalms, hymns and spiritual songs. Sing and make music in your heart to the Lord, always giving thanks to God the Father for everything, in the name of our Lord Jesus Christ. Submit to one another out of reverence for Christ. (Ephesians 5:19-21)

This next section of Ephesians, 5:1 through 6:9, reminds us of God's main goal for us, "to live a life of love, just as Christ loved us" (5:2). Paul now turns to the social implications of this faith-working-through-love pattern. The pattern will change our way of structuring relationships.

True reciprocal, intimate, Christ-centered love is profoundly rewarding, fascinating and fulfilling. Once you have tasted this true love, all other delights pale by comparison. Paul is telling us how to structure relationships so that we can experience this wonder more consistently. Three recommendations follow.

Cleansing from Sin

First, avoid the obvious sins that destroy true love, especially sexual sin. This will kill love faster than you can say "Hugh Hefner." Sexual immorality will lead us out of true love and into an imitation that can never satisfy us. Greed, obscenity and other forms of immorality are foolish wild-goose-chases that destroy people and congregations. These counterfeits keep us from the true love God designed us to enjoy.

Worshiping Together

Second, learn to address one another with thanksgiving (verses 4, 20), with psalms and hymns and spiritual songs (verse 19). In other words, relationships grow best when Jesus is the acknowledged center of them; and when people are loving and appreciating Him openly with each other. When Christians are together, they are not afraid to good-gossip about Jesus, to brag on Him at least a little. He is the center of their lives, so He is also at the center of some of their conversation.

Mutual Submission

Third, submit to each other for Jesus' sake. Like worshiping together, mutual submission is a direct result of being filled with the Spirit. The *NIV Study Bible* notes point out, "The grammar indicates that this mutual submission is associated with the filling of the Spirit in v. 18. The command 'be filled' (v. 18) is followed by a series of participles in Greek: speaking (v. 19), singing (v. 19), making music (v. 19), giving thanks (v. 20) and submitting (v. 21)."

Submitting is always a mutual thing among Christians. If Jesus alone is Lord, then mutual submission among Christians is a necessary corollary. In husband-wife relationships, parent-child relationships, and even in master-slave relationships,† no one has a right to lord it over another person. Those in headship or leadership positions must learn that Christ might use a person under them to speak His words over them. Christ died for all, therefore all have value and deserve respect, including women, children and slaves, the people who were considered "lesser" in Roman culture. But God doesn't consider any of them "lesser." We are all equal as co-heirs of the grace of life in Jesus Christ.

Humility now leads us to a social command that restructures all relationships: mutual submission. When we try to control other people, we are actually competing with Christ who wants to be their Master exclusively. Mutual submission is a key social principle in achieving unity.

The evil one loves to get people to dominate and control other people. Jesus comes in the opposite spirit and

† Paul had to deal with slavery pastorally, because this was part of the social reality in the Roman world. This does not imply acceptance of slavery.

shows us how to win peoples' hearts through voluntary humility. Paul is not saying that men should wear the pants in their families, should make sure their children obey their every wish and check to see whether their slaves are completely obedient. In each case, when dealing with Christian households, Paul is telling how men and women, parents and children, slaves and masters can enter into mutual submission.

Peace and unity are impossible without humility, and humility never dwells on our "right" to have other people obey us. Our only right as Christians is to be children of God (1 John 1:12). Humility is how a changed heart begins to transform social relationships—by bringing a whole new spirit into all relationships—and ultimately into a city.

Imagine, for instance, how Richmond might have been transformed if masters had done what Paul specifically wrote for them: "Do not threaten slaves." The entire slavery system would surely have collapsed from within if masters had listened to God's word to them. The slave system was fueled by threats and fear. But because masters were not willing to listen to their part of the mutual submission equation, our country's emergence out of slavery was far more difficult than it needed to be.

■ ■ ■

Chapter Ten

SPIRITUAL WARFARE

For our struggle is not against flesh and blood, but against the rulers, against the authorities, against the powers of this dark world.... (Ephesians 6:12)

Paul's point about mutual submission runs on through Ephesians 6:9. In verse 10, he begins perhaps the most well-known of all the passages of Ephesians. Here he describes our only real warfare: not a controversy among Christians, but a battle against dark angels.

This is why it is so tragic when Christians try to destroy each other. God wants us to stand together to fight a common enemy—Satan. A house divided against itself cannot stand in the thick of battle—and yes, we are in a battle whether we realize it or not. This fact alone should make us pause every time we speak destructively against fellow Christians.

It's All Warfare

This final section of Ephesians is actually a summary of the letter. Each piece of armor—waistcloth, breastplate, shoes, shield, helmet and sword—is something Paul has already written about in the first five-and-a-half chapters.

Spiritual warfare, in other words, is not only a matter of rebuking and binding demons. That may be part of it, but it isn't the main part. The main part is simple obedience to God's wishes, to all the revelations of wisdom that Paul has been sharing with us so far, for example:

1. Truth, Chapter 4
2. Righteousness, Chapter 5
3. The Gospel of Peace, Chapter 2:11-22
4. Faith, Chapter 2:1-10
5. Salvation (our inheritance), Chapter 1
6. The Word (revelation) of God, Chapter 3

Notice that most of this spiritual warfare is protective—it is armor. God doesn't want us to get hurt. He knows we live in a dark and hurtful world, and His main objective is to keep us safe. If we obey His wishes, the Bride of Christ won't get torn apart. God does not want the Bride to tear itself limb from limb because of the tricks of the devil.

If the Bride *does* get torn apart, it is the result of deception. There was a woman who, in the '80's, was taken over by demonic powers who convinced her that her right side was good, and her left side was evil. She was placed in the care of physicians because her right arm was constantly trying to destroy her left side—even to the point of plucking out her left eye or shredding her left arm. Eventually, the woman received deliverance, and was restored to her right mind. The Church needs just such deliverance as this.

If we want to make sure that "having done all" we the Church can "remain standing," we need more of the basics: tell the truth, believe the gospel, be at peace with each other because Jesus died for us, be moral, feed on the word of God. There may be other more refined aspects in spiritual warfare, but these are what we need, to survive in a hostile world as the Body of Christ, and to keep from devouring each other.

The goal?—the Body of Christ, speaking the truth in love, growing up in every way into Christ the Head, from whom the whole body, joined and held together by every supporting ligament, grows and upbuilds itself in love, as each part does its work.

Could we dare to believe that this could happen in Richmond, Virginia among people who come from wildly different backgrounds? Could our inheritance in Christ overcome the natural and human differences that the enemy uses to tear apart the Church at Richmond?

Part Three

■ ■ ■

BUILDING THE
CITY-WIDE
CHURCH

Chapter Eleven

THE PATTERN OF SOUND TEACHING

The Church at Richmond is a movement, not a denomination. We do not propose a bureaucracy, or a detailed set of doctrines for all Christians to subscribe to. Nor do we recommend giving up our separate identities and local congregations in favor of one massive gathering of Christians at a newly expanded Richmond Coliseum.

What we do propose is that we learn to worship, pray and work together in spite of our differences and insecurities, building relationships of trust and love. We ask that the pastors of Richmond sidestep the temptation to build ourselves up by preaching against other pastors and their traditions. We ask that all Christians pay closer attention to the pattern of sound teaching in the Word of God.

The Pattern of Sound Teaching

The scriptures are full of reminders that it is how we live, not merely how we think or preach, that God most cares about. God has given us a simple pattern and we are accountable to Him to live by it. The pattern is this: "faith working through love" (Galatians 5:6 RSV), of which Paul says, that nothing else matters.

How consistently this pattern is taught throughout our New Testament:

> *As I urged you when I went into Macedonia, stay there in Ephesus so that you may command certain men not to teach false doctrines any longer nor to devote themselves to myths and endless genealogies. These promote controversies rather than God's work—which is by faith. The goal of this command is love, which comes from a pure heart and a good conscience and a sincere faith. Some have wandered away from these and turned to meaningless talk. (1 Timothy 1:3-6)*

God wants to produce in each of us a pattern, and that pattern is the true goal of ministry: faith leading to purity of life that paves the way for genuine love. Whatever does not produce that pattern is false doctrine. Meaningless talk. The pattern is a life of love rooted in faith in Jesus. Again:

> *What you heard from me, keep as the pattern of sound teaching, with faith and love in Christ Jesus. (2 Timothy 1:13)*

John reiterates the same pattern:

And this is his command: to believe in the name of his Son, Jesus Christ, and to love one another as he commanded us. (1 John 3:23)

Most disunity among Christians comes as a simple failure to keep to this pattern. We may put a finer and nobler spin on our divisive ways, but neglecting the pattern of sound teaching is almost invariably at the base of the problem.

An Example from the West[24]

The result is often a severe loss of credibility to the good news of Christ. Examples abound in this country.

In the 18th century, there was a little known spiritual awakening that occurred among Native Americans of the Columbia Plateau—Eastern Oregon and Washington, and Northern Idaho. God began to speak to the main tribal leaders about Jesus, prior to the intrusion of any white people into the area. For example, the Flathead chief, Shining Shirt, received revelation that the Creator wanted the Flatheads to give up sister-marriage because the Creator was pleased with monogamy. He obeyed this word as soon as he heard it, and God revealed to him a shape, in the form of a cross, which was precious to the Creator. Warriors began to wear the cross as an amulet as they went into battle. The Holy Spirit revealed to Shining Shirt that God would lead men of white skin wearing black robes to teach them further what He wanted them to know about Himself.

Simultaneously, the Holy Spirit spoke to the great Spokane prophet, Circling Raven, during the first smallpox epidemic of the West. Men would come from the rising sun, men of white skin bearing "leaves bound together." They should hear what these men taught about the Creator, and pay attention to the words in the leaves bound together.

The Coeur d'Alene prophet Twisted Earth received a similar word about men of white skin and black robes; he and his father taught the Coeur d'Alenes about a great person who was born long ago, a Savior. The Creator wanted them to begin to celebrate His birth each year during the winter. They began to celebrate Christmas as an annual holy day well before any white people arrived on the scene.

"Send Us Teachers"

By 1810, the expectancy on the Columbia Plateau had risen to such a fervor that when white people did begin to show up from the east, they were pestered with requests for religious teachers who would instruct them about the Savior. In 1825, George Simpson, head of the Hudson's Bay Company's Northern District, acted upon these requests, and took two chiefs' sons with him to receive instruction at the Anglican mission post in Red River Colony (Winnipeg).

The Anglican rectors there, William Cochran and David Jones, did a good job of loving these two teenagers, Spokan Garry and Kootenai Pelly. They shared the gospel with them and baptized them. The boys returned to the Columbia Plateau in 1828, and preached the gospel to all the Plateau tribes. There was great interest in the Jesus they preached, and their preaching sparked an extraordinary furor of faith and prayer. After all, the way had been prepared by their own highly respected cultural leaders.

So successful was this initiation into Christian faith that Garry and Pelly took seven more chiefs' sons with them to be instructed at Red River.[25] Unfortunately, Kootenai Pelly died from a fall from a horse; but Spokan Garry returned to the Plateau and became a recognized preacher, respected chief and diplomat for the Plateau tribes.

Then: The Missionaries

Within the next fifteen years, the tribes succeeded in their request for white people who would teach about Jesus. It was primarily Catholic, Anglican and Presbyterian missionaries who answered this call during the1840's.

They were presented with a missionary's fondest dream: people eager for news about Jesus, because they had been prepared by their own cultural leaders.

Yet, within a few years, most Plateau peoples had turned away from Christ in large numbers. Why?

In those early hopeful years before Custer's last stand, and the disastrous experiment with Indian boarding schools, missionaries mixed into the gospel generous portions of their hostility *against each other*. Chiefs, seeing this divisive spirit, exclaimed, "We already have enough of this spirit here."

In the foreword to the biography of Spokan Garry, Dr. Herman Deutsch, Professor of History of Washington State University, summarized the early experience of area tribes with the Christian gospel:

> *"...There is abundant evidence to establish the fact that the Indian was most responsive to Christian tenets and that the native faith was not out of tune with the white man's creed. It is even more apparent that denominationalism, regardless of how essential it may be in a free society, not only militated against the Indian's integration into the Christian community but fragmented the ranks of the natives at the very time concerted action was essential in the struggle for their survival."* [26]

A weak and divided Church was unable to maintain a credible witness among Native people. The result was summarized by Dr. Ralph Winter of the U.S. Center for World Mission: "...Of the hundreds of tribal societies (in this country), not a single example exists of a truly indigenous, virile church movement. [27]

Today, after 300 years of presenting Christ to Native people in this country, barely 6% have become Christians. Of course, the reasons for this failure are complex. But we wonder how the story might have turned out differently if the Christians had simply learned how to practice toward each other the basic pattern, faith working through love.

■ ■ ■

Chapter Twelve

AVOID FOOLISH CONTROVERSIES

On the "tails" side of the coin, Paul warns us against divisiveness so many times that it becomes almost tiresome. Yet these are the most neglected commandments in the community of Christ:

But avoid foolish controversies and genealogies and arguments and quarrels about the law, because these are unprofitable and useless. Warn a divisive person once, and then warn him a second time. After that, have nothing to do with him. You may be sure that such a person is warped…. (Titus 3:9-11a)

Don't have anything to do with foolish and stupid arguments, because you know they produce quarrels. And the Lord's servant must not quarrel; instead, he must be kind to everyone…. (2 Timothy 2:23-24a)

> *I urge you, brothers, to watch out for those who*
> *cause divisions and put obstacles in your way that*
> *are contrary to the teaching you have learned.*
> *Keep away from them. For such people are not*
> *serving our Lord Christ, but their own appetites.*
> *(Romans 16:17-18a)*

Lessons from the Celtic Church

Avoiding divisive behavior is not as easy as it sounds, even though divisiveness clearly violates the pattern of sound teaching, and it is a sin against God. Consider, for example, what brought on the downfall of one of the greatest outpourings of the Spirit of God in history, that which created the community of Iona in the west of Scotland. That Christian community was created by one of the truly great saints of history, Columba, alias Columcille, a Celtic Christian who emigrated from Ireland in 563. It is said that Columba converted the Picts through a power encounter with Druid priests very much like Moses before Pharaoh. Soon, dozens of Christian communities were established throughout Scotland.

The Community at Iona quickly became the most vibrant community of believers in the world, spanning oceans to reestablish Christian communities by the hundreds throughout Europe, following the fall of Rome to the barbarians.

But one day, someone noticed an unsettling thing among these Celtic Christians in the north. They celebrated

Easter on a different day than did his own tradition in the south. Also, the Celtic leaders looked weird. Their tonsures were highly unconventional. (A tonsure, for those who may not know, is the bald spot shaved on the heads of monks.) The Christians in the south objected to the tonsures of the people in the north.

Scandalized by these irregularities, church authorities swooped up to the North and held a council to bring uniformity in things tonsural and in the matter of dates. There could not possibly be two right answers on these issues. Someone had to be wrong. So they called a council, the Synod of Whitby in 664, to decide who was right and who wrong.

Most Celtic leaders felt that these issues were not important enough to argue about, yet they found that more and more of their own people were inclined to make an issue of dates and tonsures. The Iona community became divided pro and con. A bad spirit began to pervade the place. Finally, many of the leaders went back to Ireland. The power of the community was drained away. Then Vikings came and sacked the island a century later.

But the power of the community had already been drained away by divisiveness. This was a huge tragedy for the gospel of Jesus Christ. A divisive spirit, feeding on silly controversies, destroyed the vibrancy of the gospel. The lesson: "Avoid foolish controversies."

What Is Foolishness?

But how are we to define a controversy as "foolish?" Everyone who ever picked a fight did it for what seemed like sound reasons. At the time, I am sure, tonsures and dates of holidays seemed deeply important. But what does *God* consider important?

Many controversies occur as a simple defense of our world-view. We cherish certain views and ways because we identify ourselves as "Anglo," "Native American," "African-American;" "Baptist," "Pentecostal," "Presbyterian;" "Liberal," "Charismatic," or "Evangelical." We become part of a community of like-minded people who reinforce each other's views.

When these cultures come into contact with each other, we have a simple decision to make. Will we allow our culture to be the foundation for our lives, or will we stand on Christ alone, and recognize our culture as non-foundational?

But when the bile rises, the red comes into our eyes and we conjure up a good argument to demolish all opposition, let us ask ourselves: Are you making a foundational issue out of something that does not deserve to be foundational?

For no one can lay any foundation other than the one already laid, which is Jesus Christ (1 Corinthians 3:11).

What Is Foundational?

There are some things we may need to debate,

foundational matters of great importance. Who is Jesus? What has He done for us? These are truly foundational and important to God.

But other issues are not foundational, and we are permitted a good deal of latitude as we debate those issues, speaking the truth in love, and growing up into Christ. As long as our relationship with Christ is healthy and vibrant, He will show us what to think in all other matters, and bring us all to maturity in Christ. The process may take time, but as we grow more sensitive to Him, cling to Him, speak the truth in love with each other, and practice the pattern of sound teaching, Jesus will help us deal with our differences.

Once we have a relationship with Christ, it is our relationship that guides us in these complicated situations with other Christians. Jesus, with His broad, deep, high and wide love, can infuse us with wisdom, the manifold wisdom of heaven, which allows manifold peoples – of every tribe and tongue, culture and denomination – into His presence.

Once we cross the bridge of right doctrine into a relationship with Christ, it is the relationship with Christ that we must trust for the complexities of Christian love. He Himself will show us what to do when we are confronted with multiplied styles of prayer, unfamiliar ways of interpreting scripture, and even unlovely Christian people.

Early doctrinal debates, which produced the Apostles' Creed and the Nicene Creed, centered on who Jesus is and what He does. These were legitimate doctrinal debates.

Had they not been resolved properly, our connection to the Head would have been jeopardized.

But after three or four centuries, councils like the Synod of Whitby gave doctrinal debate a bad name. In part, this was due to a false belief that Christians had to be uniform, not merely unified. In part, it was, no doubt, because certain people wanted to lord it over other people and win arguments. But at heart, it was a failure to discern between what is foundational and what is not.

A foolish controversy is one that is argued as though it were foundational when it is not foundational at all. And the foundation of the Church is Christ alone.

■ ■ ■

Chapter Thirteen

ESTEEMING ONE ANOTHER IN LOVE

The City of Richmond is full of many different kinds of churches ministering to all kinds of people. Why do we have difficulty coming together from our different corners of the city, and truly appreciating and loving each other? Is it possible to get together across denominational and racial lines—and enjoy it?

Though all of us Christians in Richmond would be considered members of the Body of Christ, all of us come from *one part* of the Body of Christ, and we carry the values and opinions that were nurtured by that part. If you are a Baptist, you think like a Baptist. If you are Pentecostal, you think Pentecostal. Your way of evaluating a Christian is a Pentecostal way, or a Presbyterian way, or a Baptist way, or a Catholic way, and so on.

But when efforts are made to put *ligaments* on the

Body of Christ, so that the different parts are learning to function together with the other parts, each part must rise up and see more broadly than it has been accustomed to do. Imagine that you are a mouth. You would esteem eloquence. If you were a hand, you would honor dexterity. An eye? Insight would be your thing. But suppose that the eye must now work in co-ordination with the hand. It must stop trying to see insight as the only thing worth living for. It must learn to honor dexterity, too. In other words, if we are to act in Richmond as the total Body of Christ, we must learn how to see things less narrowly, and not to esteem other people only by the narrow standards of our denominational culture.

He Distributes Different Gifts

Virtually every one of our denominations was born in a season of spiritual awakening in the past. During that season, God was emphasizing one or another of the riches of Christ, attempting to re-introduce it to the Body of Christ. As He did this, various denominations and groups of Christians were awakened to God at the point of that gift, and that gift became very precious to them. Let's review the basic gifts of our inheritance in Christ, as listed by Paul in Ephesians, chapter one:

1) Adoption
2) Redemption
3) Forgiveness of Sin
4) A New Purpose for Living
5) The Glory of God

6) Eternal Salvation
7) The Holy Spirit

To this day, the various denominations in our city tend to stress one aspect of this seven-fold inheritance. It is as though they have been given that one gift in trust to guard and steward it to the larger Body of Christ. In the present city-wide Church movement, what is trying to emerge is the beauty of the whole Body of Christ, equipped with every good gift and lacking nothing, with each part working properly.

Some groups in Richmond emphasize the adoptive love of the Father, others the power of the cross, others the sovereignty and glory of God, others the calling to change the world by Kingdom work, others the gift of eternal salvation, others the power of the Holy Spirit. As long as these gifts are kept separate and the parts of the Body disparage each other, the Body of Christ remains weak and ineffective. But imagine the power and authority that would emerge to transform a city if the various parts were brought together, ligaments were formed, relationships of trust grew up among the parts, and then God breathed life into the Church at Richmond.

Keeping the Other Gifts in View

At present, throughout the West, God is pouring out *Adoption*. The adoptive love of the Father is everywhere poured into broken hearts through Christian healing ministries, revival gatherings, worship ministries, the practice of "soaking" in the Father's love, and current trends in Christian music. It is not hard to see that God is moving into our troubled society full of broken homes, runaway dads and abandoned children, to heal the children's broken hearts and restore them with the Father's love.

This emphasis on the Father's adoptive love is emerging into a Church scene full of Christians who have been embracing other gifts. These Christians do not always appreciate the "new" thing God is giving. Conversely, those who have been deeply touched by the Father's love in the current movement can overlook the valuable and genuine gifts God has given to other Christians during other seasons. Will we have the breadth of perspective to step beyond our tendency to see *our* gift as the *main* gift.

Others emphasize *The Cross* and the things that flow from the cross—redemption and forgiveness. They have crucifixes hanging from their sanctuaries and rear-view mirrors; they have developed confession of sin to a fine art; and they stress the sacraments that apply the cross to our lives week after week. To them, the cross is truly central, which it must surely be for all of us. Yet the sacramental churches can also become exclusive and blind to the other gifts, while those who hold the other gifts can be blind to them.

Other Christians are full of God's call on their lives to change the world so that "His kingdom comes on earth." They are full of *God's Purpose* for this world here and now, and are tired of idle Christians who are just waiting for "pie in the sky by and by," as they are fond of saying.

They want to transform cities and societies to make them just and loving. This is as it should be—until they begin to demean others with other gifts like Sacrament, Salvation or Spirit of God.

Other Christians, consumed with fervor over the *Glory of God*, are singing that "the chief end of man is to glorify God and enjoy Him forever." They are full of the vision of God's greatness, beauty, goodness, sovereignty and majesty. This is their gift, and they are giving it to the rest of us. But it, too, can be a badge of superiority and divisiveness, and those in the other groups can rail against this group because they are "not getting anything done."

Others keep hammering away at the basic gift of *Eternal Salvation*. Their life calling is to present that gift to the unsaved and unchurched, and it is almost as if nothing else matters to them.

Others have specialized in the person and work of the *Holy Spirit*. God has clearly used them to reintroduce parts of our inheritance that had been lost to the larger Body of Christ in recent centuries.

Richard Foster

Richard Foster has helped many comprehend the variety of legitimate streams in the Body of Christ. His writings, *Streams of Living Water*[28] and *Devotional Classics*[29] elucidate six streams that have gained legitimacy from past seasons of revival: the Contemplative, Holiness, Charismatic, Justice, Evangelical and Sacramental.

Foster describes what he sees as the unique characteristic of the emerging move of God's Spirit:

The astonishing new reality in this mighty flow of the Spirit is how sovereignly God is bringing together streams of life that have been isolated from one another for a very long time. This isolation is completely understandable from a historical perspective. Over the centuries some precious teaching or vital experience is neglected until, at the appropriate moment, a person or movement arises to correct the omission. Numbers of people come under the renewed teaching, but soon vested interests and a host of other factors come into play, producing resistance to the renewal, and the new movement is denounced. In time it forms its own structures and community life, often in isolation from other Christian communities.

This phenomenon has been repeated many times through the centuries. The result is that various streams of life—good streams, important streams—have been cut off from the rest of the Christian community, depriving us all of a balanced vision of life and faith.

But today our sovereign God is drawing many streams together that heretofore have been separated from one another. It is a little like the Mississippi River, which gains strength and volume

*as the Ohio and the Missouri and many other rivers
flow into it. So in our day God is bringing together
a mighty "Mississippi of the Spirit."*[30]

Perhaps the unique characteristic of the emerging move of
God in the twenty-first century is just this: God is
challenging us to appreciate and fully explore all the riches
of Christ as He has distributed them to various groups of
Christians who still today hold them in trust for the whole
Body of Christ. The words of Jesus in the parable of the
pounds take on new meaning:

*A nobleman went into a far country to receive a
kingdom and then return. Calling ten of his
servants, he gave them ten pounds, and said to
them, 'Trade with these until I come.'" (Luke
19:12-13)*

This command to "trade" implies that we will be willing
to give to and receive from each other.

■ ■ ■

Chapter Fourteen

THE ART OF PLAYING BRIDGE

Bridge is a game that requires great skill—the learned ability to discern your partner's strong suit without seeing her hand. Then you have to use her strong suit to help win the game. Inexperienced players often think that their own hand alone is the key to winning the game. Players like that *almost always lose*.

We Christians have an opponent, but he is not each other. Other Christians are our partners in God's game of bridge. Satan is the opponent.

If we wish to win the game, we will have to learn how to play by the rules and techniques God recommends—and that includes learning how to play *as partners*. At first, we play stupidly because we are inexperienced. We get mad at our partner's stupid plays, get alienated from her and then ignore her cards entirely.

Some Christians in "other" traditions do play foolishly, and we feel justified in being irritated at them. But it is only by learning how to play the game as partners that we will ever gain the skills required to master the game as partners. In the meantime, we have to learn to be patient with each other. The key to winning God's game is still the same: discerning the other Christian's strong suit, and utilizing it in the play of the game.

Playing Bridge; Building Bridges

Some leaders in Richmond are learning to do this very thing. Pastor Wayne Mancari of Cornerstone Assembly of God has been learning this bridge-playing skill. Seven years ago, he began to reach out to pastors of different traditions than his own. He calls on them in their offices, one a week, to get acquainted with them. As he does, he finds out what excites them, what their gift and vision is, and then prays for them at his church each Sunday. By building bridges in this way, he is gaining a real appreciation for the full variety of strengths in the Body of Christ in Richmond.

Chuck Crismier, host of the radio broadcast, "The Richmond Connection," has opened his home periodically for the last several years, inviting pastors of all traditions to come together over dinner—dozens at a time—to get acquainted and share their hearts with each other. Out of these gatherings, pastor-to-pastor hospitality groups have been forming, in which four pastoral couples commit themselves to long-term relationships through the gift of hospitality. They open their homes to each other and share a meal together regularly. Through this acquired habit, pastoral friendships have had time to grow up across age-old lines of division that have separated Christians for years. In gatherings like these, we can discover each other's strong suit.

Pressing Through Until We Connect

In these budding relationships, we may at first be appalled at each other's differences. If we don't realize that God wants us to work at love, we will turn aside from the love commandment too soon. But it is usually only the external things that prove to be alienating. The inheritance that God ministers into our hearts has the opposite effect. The inheritance unites. Those who have the pattern of faith working through love succeed in pressing through to the heart-and-spirit level of conversation. A skillful host can gently guide the conversation away from successful building programs or the size of our last new members' class to sharing stories of how we have come, or are coming, to know Christ more fully. Clinging to God, we find the strength to break through the walls of denominational competitiveness and stereotyping to discover the heart-connections that might be described as "ligaments."

The result? God bonds us together in Christ. The King asserts Himself. In the end, we think, "How could I have had such negative thoughts about this person? I called him a "counterfeit"—or one of "those denominational

Christians," or one of "the holy rollers." They are Christians just as we are!

Overcoming Difficulties

In the process of forming these ligaments, we will likely have to confront the bug-a-boo that prevented us from reaching out to each other in the first place: areas of disagreement and offense.

Let us imagine a new sort of "city-wide" Christian in Richmond—one who is adjusting to the concept of "The Church at Richmond." These are the things he would be likely to say to a Christian from another tradition as he deals with controversies and offenses:

1. I Can Spit Out the Bones.

"To be frank, not everything in your life and tradition is helpful to me. No offense, but this is how it is. There are things you believe and practice that, in my heart of hearts, I think are misguided. Perhaps these things are just for you, not for me. But that is not going to stop me from opening the pantry door to find out what good things God has given you that you could give me.

"None of us is perfect. When I see my own imperfections, I am then free to let you be imperfect too. Actually, I don't hold your imperfections against you. If I did, I'd have to answer to the Lord, who says, 'judgment without mercy will be shown to all those who are not merciful'

(James 2:13). I want to feed on the food God gave you for me, but I reserve the right to spit out the bones. As long as you give me the right to discern for myself what is meat and what is bones, I am free to eat of you to my heart's content."

2. I Can Learn How to Get under Your Skin.

"I think I could give you a gift Jesus gave me. But as long as there is a wall between us, I can't give it to you. You would have to learn to trust me before you would let me give you my gift. So I am going to build up my relationship with you, just because I care about you. Maybe one day, I will be able to impart to you something good God gave me.

"But if I am harsh with you, you aren't going to let me get under your skin, to tap into your veins. You're going to close off your heart from me. When people talk at me with harshness or with a condescending attitude, I never listen to them. Why should I expect you to be any different with me? Therefore, every attempt I make to impart a piece of truth to you, I will do with love and gentleness. That's my only hope of doctoring your heart with anything intravenous that will bless you."

3. I Won't Carry Offenses. Please Don't Do the Same with Me.

"If you are offended or hurt, I ask you to come to me and tell me. If I am offended, I will come to you. Offense will be taken care of as soon as possible. I promise not to let bitterness linger, because bitterness will 'defile many.'"[31]

4. We Can "Walk in the Opposite Spirit."

"As I look at the sins of this city, I will avoid the temptation to believe that I am not a part of the city and participating in its sin. I refuse to speak easy judgments or to call down fire on the city. Instead, when I see someone else's sin, I will examine my own life, to earnestly see if that same sin resides in my own heart. Then I will set my heart to live in the opposite spirit from those I know to be misguided or wrong."

What is the goal of all this care, patience, forbearance and upbuilding love? We are working our way to the place where we want someone else's ministry to succeed as much as, or even more than, our own. To begin with, we see how the other Christian's emphasis fits into the total picture of what Christ is building here. But beyond that, we can even see that God wants us to walk in the opposite spirit to the "spirit of this age." He wants us to walk in love.

This is unity lifestyle, a lifestyle that will enable us to walk worthily of the calling to which we have been called as one Body.

■ ■ ■

Chapter Fifteen

LIVING THE HIGH PRIEST'S PRAYER

As the third millennium gets underway, we sense an urgency about Jesus' High Priestly prayer—"that all of them (the believers) may be one" (John 17:21).

It is impossible to imagine that the end of the age could come upon us without the prayer of Jesus having been fulfilled, and the Body of Christ rising to its true Bridal potential. Surely the fledgling efforts at Christian unity emerging today are a result of Jesus' own longings and prayers.

Seymour's Faith

William Seymour, the African-American leader of the Azusa Street Revival, believed that the profound unity that marked that Revival was a sign that Jesus was coming back soon. In that Revival, people from every known culture in

Los Angeles, a truly polyglot city, were pulled together with a wonderful love and unity straight from the heart of God.

Unfortunately, the curtain came crashing down on this scene when Seymour's mentor, a Ku Klux Klan sympathizer, arrived on the scene and rebuked them all for mingling the races. As Harvey Cox pointed out in his review of the astonishing emergence of the Pentecostal churches a century ago, white pastors began to pull away from Seymour[32] As a result, the Pentecostal denominations that emerged from that Revival were racially segregated.

Will God give Richmond an opportunity to complete what God began in Los Angeles a century ago? Jesus is the Alpha *and* the Omega. He always finishes what He begins. Will He find a people here willing to stand against the demonic forces that still divide the Church in this country?

New Beginnings

If so, then we must find visible expressions of unity that gain the confidence of our community—of the churched and the unchurched alike. Efforts have been underway, and we will summarize what we are seeing at the time of this writing. There may be other efforts we are not aware of. Still other efforts may grow up soon after this book is published—such efforts are proliferating rapidly. We give the specifics we know about, so that those who are becoming energized by the vision of a city-wide Church can get involved in what is already happening.

• *The Family Policy Council,* headed by Dr. James

Anderson, and supported by business leaders in Richmond, seeks to facilitate relationship building and develop trust among pastors, youth pastors, the business community and health-care workers—trust that transcends racial and denominational differences. The Council has also developed a communication network within the Christian community, facilitates an annual Pastor's Prayer Breakfast on the National Day of Prayer each May, and works in public high schools and middle schools to promote abstinence education among teens. Finally, Dr. Anderson has worked with Pastor Randy Bremer and Colley Burton at St. Giles Presbyterian Church to host monthly breakfasts for pastors. Call James Anderson at 804-276-9305, ext. 221 for more information or e-mail him at jcanderson@homerelay.net. Or call St. Giles Presbyterian Church for information about the breakfast, 282-9763.

• *Jesus Day* is a tried and true expression of Christian unity to enable the Body of Christ to worship Jesus publicly in Richmond (along with many other cities throughout the world). During Jesus Day, the Saturday before Pentecost, Richmond churches are encouraged to co-operate in an outreach to the poor, then all believers are invited to praise-walk Broad Street from Chimborazo Park to the State Capitol during the afternoon. Outreach projects are arranged at other times of the year, as well. Try the Jesus Day website, www.jesusday-richmond.org. Call Chris and Jeanine Guidry at 804-745-7824 or e-mail JesusDay@att.net.

- *The Richmond Connection* is a weekly radio broadcast that informs and inspires Christians to pray and work for the transformation of Richmond. Host Chuck Crismier interviews many of those who have a heart for the vision presented in this book. Tune in to the broadcast which, at the time of this writing, takes place on Saturday, 9 to 9:30 a.m. on WBTK, AM 1380; and Sunday 3 to 3:30 p.m. on WGGM, AM 820. Chuck has developed a website at richmondconnection.org. He also works to create covenantal relationships through Pastor-to-Pastor hospitality ministry. Call Chuck at 804-754-1822.

- *Marriage Builders Alliance* is a pastor-led effort to build and maintain healthy marriages in Richmond. A diverse representation of pastors has signed a covenant to stem the tide of divorce in this city. By coming together across racial, doctrinal and denominational lines, Christian leaders in several cities nationwide have greatly impacted the divorce rate in their cities. Why not Richmond? View their website: www.MarriageBuildersAlliance.org or contact Bob Ruthazer, 804-282-9763, ext. 13.

- *Needle's Eye Ministries* is an outreach to Richmond's marketplace. It offers monthly luncheons, weekly small groups, Christian Presidents' Groups, an outreach to spiritually searching GenXers (Spiritual Shots™), sponsorship of an online *Faith & Values* channel, seminars, mission trips and special events. View their website: www.needleseye.org or contact Buddy

Childress at 804-358-1283.

- *Common Thread* is an intercessory ministry working to unite Christians in prayer for Richmond. Matthew and Sherrie Moore are using the "Harp and Bowl" model developed by the International House of Prayer in Kansas City, to encourage 24/7 prayer for Richmond. Common Thread also organizes seasons of prayer and fasting, enlisting churches to participate twice a year. These PrayRichmond seasons often include an interdenominational communion service. Call Matthew and Sherrie at 804-560-7040.

- *Richmond Hill* is an ecumenical Christian community with residential and non-residential members from more than 10 Christian denominations located in the historic Monastery of the Sisters of the Visitation of Monte Maria on the crest of the hill where William Byrd laid out the City of Richmond. Since 1988, the Community has joined in prayer three times daily for the transformation of Metropolitan Richmond. These prayer services at 7 a.m., 12 noon, and 6 p.m. are open to the public. Richmond Hill maintains a retreat center for individuals and groups, and offers courses and schools in Spiritual Guidance, Christian Healing Prayer, Christian Formation, Pastoral Care and Counseling, and Racial, Jurisdictional, and Economic Issues of Metropolitan Richmond. For more information, try www.RichmondHillVa.org, visit Richmond Hill at 2209 East Grace Street, or call 804-783-7903 and talk to the Rev. Benjamin P.

Campbell, Pastoral Director, the Rev. Janie Walker, Associate Pastor for Individual Ministry, or another member of the Community.

- *Christian Ministries United* (www.cmu-richmond. org), headed by Lyle Thomas, is a coalition of over 60 local nonprofit organizations that helps foster relationships and trade resources between ministries, congregations, and other parts of the Body of Christ for strategic initiatives. Out of that ministry *Transformation Richmond* has grown up, a fellowship of Christian leaders, many of whom are mentioned on these pages, who are working toward the broad vision articulated in this book. Transformation Richmond, in turn, sponsors the *Richmond Prayer Summit*, a four-day event in which pastors meet to seek God for our city. The CMU number is 804-359-5357. Transformation Richmond and the Prayer Summit are accessed through the website: www.transformationrichmond.org.

- *The Urban Ministries Hotline*, created and managed by Gwen Mansini, is pulling together people from all over the city who minister to the poor. Gwen has also been instrumental in developing the Richmond Outreach Center, which pulls volunteers from dozens of Richmond churches to meet the physical and spiritual needs of people. The Center, pastored by Geronimo Aguilar, has the potential to be a model for co-operative ventures like it all over Richmond. Get in touch with Gwen at MCCSEC1@aol.com and she will add you to the hotline. Check out the ROC at www.RichmondOutreachCenter.com.

Transformation Richmond

These leaders and groups have learned to work by consensus, esteeming one another in love. They have built a bedrock of relationships, trusting each other through difficulties and they are laboring in Richmond for the long haul. This Transformation Richmond team has developed a sonar system to spot lone rangers—people who believe that God has appointed them to transform this city single-handedly. They are trying to develop a lifestyle of mutual submission out of reverence for Christ.

These relationships have grown up at considerable cost and investment over the years. Those who are enjoying the fruits of this investment are now turning to other Christians and saying: Won't you join us in the higher vision of a city-wide Church in our city?

Those who wish to do further reading along these lines are invited to read Jack Dennison's book, *City Reaching*, and to watch the two "Transformations" videos available from Lyle Thomas at CMU headquarters or from George Otis at www.sentinelgroup.org. In an effort to encourage participation in this increasing network of city-wide ministries, we hope to publish a list of them each year, to distribute to all who are curious about, or even excited about the vision of this book, so that Christians can plug in wherever the Holy Spirit might lead them.

Dry Bones, Bride of Christ

We believe that the Church is supposed to be God's instrument of transformation for our city. A prayerless and divided Church cannot be such an instrument. Something must happen to us like the prophecy of dry bones given to Ezekiel:

> *I will attach tendons to you,*
> *And make flesh come upon you,*
> *And cover you with skin.*
> *I will put breath in you,*
> *And you will come to life. (Ezekiel 37:6)*

This prophecy has four parts and a conclusion:

- The "tendons" or ligaments are relationships. God brings forth relationships of love among Christians, who connect to each other and learn to trust each other.

- The "flesh" is incarnational ministry, God-anointed ministry that flows out of God-appointed relationships.

- "Skin" is what covers the whole, giving wholeness and unity to all the working parts. Also, it adds the beauty factor. A whole and united Church is beautiful, "a bride pure and spotless."

- "Breath" is the power of the Spirit of God like that which was poured into the united, praying Church at Jerusalem on the Day of Pentecost.

And then, the conclusion: "You will come to life." Dare we believe this promise for the Church at Richmond?

■ ■ ■

NOTES

1 Jack Dennison, *City Reaching: On the Road to Community Transformation* (Pasadena: William Carey Library, 1999), p. 13.

2 Jacques Ellul: *The Meaning of the City* (Grand Rapids: Eerdmans, 1970).

3 The miracle of Mizoram is described briefly by George Otis, Jr. in *Informed Intercession* (Ventura, CA: Gospel Light, 1999), pp. 16-18.

4 Jonathan Goforth, *When the Spirit's Fire Swept Korea* (Grand Rapids: Zondervan, 1943), pp. 10-11.

5 *The Secret Diary of William Byrd of Westover 1709-1712*, Louis B. Wright and Marion Tinling, eds. (Richmond: Dietz, 1941).

6 Virginius Dabney, *Richmond: The Story of a City* (Charlottesville: University Press of Virginia, 1990), pp. 9, 12.

7 *Ibid*, pp. 11.

8 Iain Murray, *Revival and Revivalism: The Making and Marring of American Evangelicalism 1750-1858* (Edinburgh: Banner of Truth, 1994), pp. 7-8.

9 *Ibid.*, p. 81.

10 *Ibid.*, p. 73.

11 *Richmond Times-Dispatch*, Sunday, March 5, 2000, p. A-1.

12 *New World Dictionary of the American Language* (N.Y. : William Collins, 1980).

13 *Save America Updates*, July, 1995, p. 7.

14 *Richmond Intercessors*, Aug. 2001, Vol. 3 #1, p. 6.

15 Charles Crismier III, "Martyr's Widow Speaks to Richmond."

16 The story is recounted more fully in Zeb Bradford Long and Douglas

McMurry, *Receiving the Power* (Grand Rapids: Chosen, 1994).

17 *Revival and Revivalism*, p. 118-119.

18 *Revival and Revivalism,* p. 120

19 "A Thanksgiving Revival Message," e-mail dated November 27, 2002 from Bob Lowman of the Metrolina Prayer Network. Used by permission.

20 E-mail message, Rauno Kokkola to Douglas McMurry, Jan. 20, 2003.

21 "Cursed be the man who keepeth back his sword from blood," *Colonial Williamsburg*, Winter, 2002-3, p. 34.

22 Peter Marshall and David Manuel, *Sounding Forth the Trumpet* (Grand Rapids: Fleming H. Revell, 1997), pp. 61-117.

23 *Revival and Revivalism*, p. 2.

24 The material in this section was based on voluminous research at the Library of Congress. Original sources are footnoted in my book, *The Collapse of the Brass Heaven*, Chapter 18. See Zeb Bradford Long and Douglas McMurry *The Collapse of the Brass Heaven* (Grand Rapids: Chosen, 1994).

25 Unfortunately, later boarding schools did such a poor job of conveying the love of Jesus that all the ground gained by Rev. Cochran and Rev. Jones was lost. Today, Canadian churches are embroiled in lawsuits stemming from child abuse in later boarding schools mandated by the government and run by churches. This was a huge disaster.

26 *Chief Spokan Garry 1811-1892, Christian, Statesman, and Friend of the White Man*, (Minneapolis: Denison, 1960), p. 5.

27 Ralph D. Winter, editorial, *Mission Frontiers*, Sept., 2000, Vol. 22, No. 4, p.4.

28 Richard Foster, *Streams of Living Water* (San Francisco: Harper, 1998).

29 Richard J. Foster and James Bryan Smith, ed., *Devotional Classics* (San Francisco: Harper, 1990).

30 *Streams of Living Water*, p. xv.

31 Hebrews 12:15.

32 Harvey Cox, *Fire From Heaven: The Rise of Pentecostal Spirituality and the Reshaping of Religion in the 21st Century* (Cambridge, MA: Da Capo Press, 2001).

OTHER BOOKS BY DOUGLAS MCMURRY

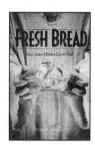

Fresh BREAD: How Jesus Draws Us to God. Written for Christians of all denominational backgrounds who are involved in discipling new believers or seekers in small groups. Can be used as a follow-up for Alpha groups. Basic Christianity freshly articulated. $9.43

FOOD GROUPS. Good follow-up guide for BREAD groups. Theme: basic Faith, Love and Holiness, the main ingredients of Christian living. Each section of 12 weeks can be studied separately from the other two. More intensive Biblical study than Fresh Bread. $5.75

Value Your Mate by Douglas McMurry and C. Everett Worthington. For couples' devotions, marriage renewal groups, or for people going through marriage counseling. How to apply the basic pattern of "Faith Working Through Love" to marriages.

(Published by Baker Books) $9.43

The Collapse of the Brass Heaven by Brad Long and Douglas McMurry. Shows why the Western Church must return to a reliance on the power of God.

(Published by Chosen Books)..............$11.49

Receiving the Power by Brad Long and Douglas McMurry. Instructs how to open our lives to the power of the Holy Spirit without being divisive, drawing on the teaching of R.A. Torrey. Points to a new era of unity of the Spirit among Christians.

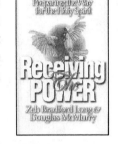

(Published by Chosen) $11.49

Prayer That Shapes the Future by Brad Long and Douglas McMurry. A vision for prayer in building the Kingdom of God.

(Published by Zondervan) $9.43

Virginia Residents add 4.5% sales tax.

Available from Bethlehem Books
Phone orders: (804) 285-0223
Or order by internet at www.Christprez.org